Sleep ⸲ You ⸲ a Tree
E.D. Blodgett

THE UNIVERSITY
of ALBERTA PRESS

APOSTROPHES VII

Sleep ⸳ You ⸳ a Tree
E.D. Blodgett

Published by
The University of Alberta Press
Ring House 2
Edmonton, Alberta, Canada T6G 2E1

Copyright © 2011 E.D. Blodgett

LIBRARY AND ARCHIVES CANADA
CATALOGUING IN PUBLICATION
Blodgett, E. D. (Edward Dickinson), 1935–
  Apostrophes VII : sleep, you, a tree
/ E.D. Blodgett.

(Currents, a Canadian literature series)
Poems.
ISBN 978-0-88864-554-8
1. Title. II. Series: Currents (Edmonton, Alta.)
PS8553.L56A667 2011   C811'.54
C2010-908140-4

All rights reserved.
First edition, first printing, 2011.
Copyedited by Peter Midgley.
Printed and bound in Canada by
Friesens, Altona, Manitoba.

A volume in (cuRRents),
a Canadian literature series.
Jonathan Hart, series editor.

"North" was previously published in *La Traductière.
Revue franco-anglaise de poésie et art visuel* (2006),
no. 24.

No part of this publication may be produced, stored in a retrieval system, or transmitted in any forms or by any means, electronic, mechanical, photocopying, recording, or otherwise, without the prior written consent of the copyright owner or a licence from The Canadian Copyright Licensing Agency (Access Copyright). For an Access Copyright licence, visit www.accesscopyright.ca or call toll free: 1–800–893–5777.

The University of Alberta Press is committed to protecting our natural environment. As part of our efforts, this book is printed on Enviro Paper: it contains 100% post-consumer recycled fibres and is acid- and chlorine-free.

The University of Alberta Press gratefully acknowledges the support received for its publishing program from The Canada Council for the Arts. The University of Alberta Press also gratefully acknowledges the financial support of the Government of Canada through the Book Publishing Industry Development Program (BPIDP) and from the Alberta Foundation for the Arts for its publishing activities.

Canadä Canada Council   Conseil des Arts
         for the Arts   du Canada

 Alberta Foundation for the Arts

Pro Tibi

TALKING	1		ARIA	26
APPLE	2		FIGURES	27
ANABASIS	3		COSMOS	28
FOOTSTEPS	4		APPEARANCES	29
DISAPPEARING	5		UNSEEN	30
SENTENCE	6		FACES	32
ABANDONED	7		WALKING	33
DANCE	8		TRACES	34
UNKNOWING	9		TEARS	36
HOUSE	10		EVERYWHERE	37
SURRENDERING	11		DRIFTING	38
INFINITY	13		SKIES	39
SWEET PEAS	14		AIR	40
RECONNAISSANCE	15		PETALS	41
LOVERS	16		SHADOWING	42
BREATHING	17		IMMENSITY	43
SETTING SUNS	18		OFFERING	44
SONGS	19		GIFT	45
DUST	20		SINGING STONES	46
SMILE	22		FIRE BIRDS	47
COLLAPSING	23		SISTERS	48
PALINGENESIS	24		TREE	49
DIALOGUE	25		RIFT	50

Contents

SHADES	51
TRACKS	52
BARED	54
DANCED	55
PICTURES	57
AFTERNOON	58
PEBBLES	59
FIELD	60
FOLLOWING	63
NORTH	64
SAYING GOD	67
HEARING GREEN	68
ACCOMPANIMENTS	69
PRAIRIE	71
WIND	73
WAKES	74
SCREAM	75
TOMBEAU	76
GODS OR	77
FACES	78

Ὁ ὕπνος σὲ τύλιξε, σὰν ἕνα δέντρο.
(Sleep bent around you, like a tree.)

—GEORGE SEFERIS

TALKING

Sometimes you make your way through many words until you reach the last
and that one fails, a sentence that has no period, it concludes
but does not end, and all the words that you have spoken wait upon
the air, attentive, and the room gives up its ordinary cast,
the light upon the chairs suddenly eager, breath given a pause.
Finally they fall about us, scattered on the floor: it is as snow
might fall, petals or the seeds that flutter down at summer's end,

invisible but brushing past us in their passage on your breath.
It could be said your sentence was a tree where branches sprouted, leaves
appeared and fruit almost where birds might come to sing in their content,
birds that are not possible to see, but in their music so
beside us that the notes of what they sing become the primal theme
of what it was you said, the fruit that did not ripen, in its place
a room and all that it contains surrendered, gardens on your tongue.

APPLE

In you apples flower, spring in infinite repose appears,
the whiteness of it on the trees almost a late winter snow
that does not fall but opens, silence that begins to fill you with
a fragrance where apples start to dream upon the branches, dreams
that enter you asleep with snow and flowers and the sun that hides
inside them, a sun of seed and flesh. How many seasons we possess,
the dream we thought we dreamt, an apple that appears to hang upon

the branch, its shape the shape of all the suns that have gone down into
the west, hanging in the sky behind the trees, the sky on fire
before they disappear, the smaller suns of apples golden in
their light, the apple that we dreamt another light, unperturbed
by day and night. Blindness cannot have dominion where we are,
nor snow deceive us hanging on the trees, or seasons, darkness or —:
but where we lie upon the grass, light is the sleep upon our flesh.

ANABASIS

We were lying under trees, beneath the skies, the stars, the leaves
above us moving in the breeze that we exhaled with every word
we spoke. They did not flutter but kept time with us, and if the phrase
went on, intent to reach the skies before it came to rest, so
the leaves began to dance in longer arcs before returning to
wherever they had been when we lay down without a word beneath
the trees, but now they were awake, leaves without the heaviness

of summer afternoons when all the air is dead, and you might see
them almost lifting with us, ready for the stars. And so it was
that what we had to say became transparent—you could see the leaves
but through the words, and you could see the stars, the skies, even the air
where they passed on, rising with our breath, the suddenness of all
of it not something we could see at last, but something that could now
see us, held in the sight of stars, the leaves translating us, and we

could not say what we had become, or if we were something at all,
a place where light passed through and no more palpable than air which for
the moment was the only skin that we might wear, and when the leaves
began to move in their desire to rise up with us, the air
that passed between them and whatever place we thought was ours was
the air we saw was our flesh, and we were of the dance they made,
the arc of it thrown out among the stars, all desire air.

FOOTSTEPS

Before they reached the ground, your footsteps paused in the late summer light
and when they settled in the grass, what we heard was that of sound
transparent, something of a sound that had already risen up
into the trees and disappeared from sight. Annunciations, when
they happen, seem to leave before we know that they have been, and all
that they contain is heard as echoes of themselves, and when they stand
as angels in the ear, we know that absence is about to drop,

but not like stones—but leaves, a single leaf that falls into the light
and all the air around it open, a mouth so surprised that when
it opens cannot help but sigh, the leaf suspended in its sigh.
We are given no more than this—: a leaf that, as it falls, offers
all that is not there for us to see, and we are its grass
where it comes down, the light behind it closed, and if it happened, it
was something held between the grass and us, an angel come and gone.

DISAPPEARING

When the rain had gone, the earth exhaled—: you would not have thought I saw
you as you were another afternoon upon a chair that rose
above your head and all your bones had fallen deeper in your flesh,
more invisible than ever when you breathed, the light that fell
upon your face autumnal, memories of summer falling through
it straying briefly on your face before they disappear, children too far
to hear. I might have reached into the air as if the only joy

of fall were taking all of it in hand, the children that we were,
the summers and the light, and all of it would have spilled over, stars
that are always outside, the where of where they are unable to
be grasped, their brightness hidden in the sun and hidden in your bones.
Knowledge is not for us, content with rain, whatever rises from
the darkness of the earth, taking it in without the slightest thought,
where it resumes in us. Its transience now ours, we stand up and look.

SENTENCE

I did not know when I was young, walking through that endless spring
and gazing at the trees their leaves just barely green, the freshness of
the air that was the freshness of my skin, I did not know the leaves
were leaves but not the leaves I thought they were but leaves already you,
the words that you were speaking into spring, the shape of trees the what
of what you said, and in me other trees stood up, not known where they
were taking root, a silent garden of the mind where leaves come forth

and stay and fall, their seasons bright beneath the rain and sun, each leaf
a syllable of that unending sentence that began before
I could remember what the spring in its initial rising might have been,
but something for me spoke, its voice without a sound and rising through
my flesh, the colour of it almost green, a voice that gathers mine
in it—: in our talking absence is not known, the sentence never
falters, both of us its voice, and we the leaves that rise and fall.

ABANDONED

No one can qualify the moon, the light that does not spring from fire
of its own that floats careless into the larger emptiness
and makes the stars turn paler where it moves, the moon that gives itself
to us in all the nakedness it is, the moon whose light is all
we have when we would wish to see into the dark, a light that is
not possible without the openness that is an absolute,
no stone that is not turned to light, and what is given us to see

is not its crescents, fullness, and its fresh nubility that comes
and goes without its knowledge—: what we call the moon is everything
abandoned, careless of its fragility, the self of it laid by
without a thought, the way your throat lies open in the dark when you
are lying next to me asleep. Moonlight gathers there, it fills
your throat with what is, and you and it so unpossessed that you,
no matter how embraced, could not be grasped, turning with the stars.

DANCE

I dreamt that when I spoke to you that I was hanging from a post,
suspended from a golden cord and covered by the sky. You asked
what held me so, the light that emanated from the cord too bright
for me to see what you might be, your voice alone filling my ears.
Who are you, who are you? you asked, and I replied, I am you as you
might be if you were hanging in the air, the post that holds you to
the ground unmoving and yet moving with whatever breeze springs up

beneath the sky: it is not possible for us to live apart
from things as they take shape against the ground, the sky, the dance that we
are moving in, the where where you have been now mine, now yours, the turns
it takes given to us to make, and our making only as
we are the dance, leaving behind whatever place we might have held
upon the ground, the dance unmoving only if its giving up
is not turned over, you where I am held against the open sky.

UNKNOWING

The berries of the mountain ash were barely visible within
the window-frame, sometimes going out of sight whenever the wind
sprang up, a dance without profundity. You might have thought them stars
the way they hung in clusters for a season, then to fall or to
be plucked away by passing birds. No one remembers when this dance
began, the slow andante in our eyes, their disappearance and
return as intimate as breath that we have known since we began

to see, the nearest that we think of what we think is infinite:
so we recognize the fading stars that move beyond our window
through the night, and so since we were young we were becoming stars
unknown to us, the night around us but as children without eyes
to know the night as our room its windows giving us the us
that is of all that is of light, of dark, the only dance, the dance
that moves between what we can see and not, eyes at home in fire.

HOUSE

Leaves had drifted up against the fence. Over the house the moon
rose and stayed till the end of night when one by one the stars went out.
The light that fell around it sheathed it in a way that we had never
seen, and should you touch it now, you would not know the wall beneath
your hands—something would give way—and should you enter it, you would
not enter any house we knew, but bare light unadorned.
Is it for this they told us that the moon was not a stone, but what

a goddess is when she puts on the shape of light to stand beside
us in the night, no other way to see her, the untouchable
that gives herself to us when light is all the house we have, the flesh
we thought was ours hers as far as night extends? The leaves against
the fence have fallen from the moon, the fence transparent where it leans
against the sky, the night beside the stars, the darkness visible
where she, alone on the waters of the air, drifts, taking us home.

SURRENDERING

You walked across the winter fields. The trees stood on the margins, full
of stillness that their branches uttered, snow lying on each of them
as if their only calling was to be the shape of snow beside
the field, and on the snow and on the branches birds stood and stared
into air and into emptiness, nothing in sight but snow,
the whiteness of it an infinity, and there you walked at home
as you could be, the scene of winter that can represent no more

than what it is, its austerities of birds and trees and snow
the all it is allowed to be. Here is what it is to be
without a way, the only footsteps those that we have made and tracks
of animals that now have disappeared, leaving after them
the silence that they made in passing. Words will not be able to
recall them, nor the trees so precise as they were, the ragged sleeves
of snow above us, birds as thin as icons on the sky. All

that seems to live in such a ritual is our moving through
it, leaving other tracks of silence in our wake, our hands embraced,
a gesture that is all the way we have—not back or forth but there
where fingers seek themselves across the snow, the place of where they touch
the one place given to them. Possibly birds understand,
the trees beneath their feet receive it and the snow awakens in
the late light surrendering its silence as one gives up a ghost.

INFINITY

Walking through winter is not a walk across infinity: how can
you tell how great the steps and how your breathing moves, and how the trees
upon horizons stand, towering over us? If we should choose
to speak, would words, like music of the spheres, surround us so with sound
that all inflection would be blurred? We are so young in this place
that we might stumble and never be heard of after. The infinite,
where we are drawn, is that hypothesis that cannot be at home

in our tongue, a language too minute to speak of what the small
might be, other than the almost silence of our breathing into our mouths,
a small that has a rhythm that is carried into space, its grandeur
all that we can give, and in the winter air the whiteness of
it semblance of the thing we think infinity might be, the start
of it an echo of that other breath that God might have exhaled
when stars burst forth and suns fell out in space invisible to us.

SWEET PEAS

You have a way of looking through a window in the early light
as if nothing that you saw belonged to you, the trees mere
accidents within your eyes, and so I cannot know if when
music ends and flowers hanging off a fence open in
the silence that has settled on the air, open you might say
for the first time and all the colours of their petals leaping high
into the air to reach the sun that comes to hold them, if they are

within your sight, yet nothing is there to hold them in their silence but
barest air, all of it then invisible inside you, the world
in flower there and seen by none, and you would think fragility
might make them weep if other flowers, deep among the stars, were not
upon another fence unseen, echoes of their fragility
no more than what you see of stars when night hangs over you, the dark
alone beheld around them, flowers gone from sight upon the air.

RECONNAISSANCE

In the end there may not be a god in sight, and you may turn
around and see no trees, no blades of grass, the sun no longer yours
to turn into a word, and things so perfectly invisible
that every object, every book you held between your fingers now
turns in the sun's orbit, a world beside yours invisible
as snow that falls through white clouds. How are we to know that all
the fragments of our deeds that came upon us unawares, your standing

in a doorway just before you disappeared, my arm waving behind
you in the empty air, the stars unseen and turning through their spheres—
how are we to know where all these moments are together held, to lie
upon the falling petals of the stars? Not to see the god
is when we know that dreams are fragments, what we know is how the dream
appears to take shape, all our knowledge dreaming, the doors, the hands,
all that we thought belonged to us adrift and waiting to be dreamt.

LOVERS

Apple trees are for lovers, all who stand beside the streams and keep
the watches of the night, the moon rising larger in your eyes,
waiting for the shells of petals floating past, all the waters of
the streams white with messages that you drink in, bodies full
of what the trees are shedding. Nothing seems alive for them: the birds
that glide through twilight sometimes singing are without sound, attuned
only to the moon consuming them, and fallen flowers, and

the streams that lose their murmurs in the grass beneath their feet, the flesh
that has been known unfelt wherever darkness touches them in its
embrace, and all stretch forth their arms to grasp the night that holds them and
apple trees that lay down the snows of their mortality, the air
alive for lovers who would seem to have become the silence that
stands up beside the streams, the silence where the night comes from, the moon
holding them all becoming flowers one by one upon the streams.

BREATHING

A rain was falling through the lilacs, falling almost soundlessly,
the long expansion of its passage from the clouds a distance full
of memory that gathered birds and blue refractions settling on
the flowers nodding in the breeze, and when the rain began to yield
to lighter air, the sun appeared. This is the eye of God, you thought,
that opens here prismatic through the lilacs, all divinity
suspended in a drop of rain. It is enough to breathe to know

the fragrance of remembered lilacs and the rain across the air:
so God must be remembered now—not his eye which the rain seemed
to carry through the lilac burdened air, but God that is without
a sign of flesh, when deep within the night you wake and know that you
are not where you have gone to sleep and over you familiar smells
of lilacs fall through winter in a landscape where the birds have all
departed, rain falling slowly through your mind, the air awake.

SETTING SUNS

Every sunset is the first and last: who can conceive the next?
It lies upon the field that stretches out before it, remotest bluffs
of trees are touched, the rocks that line the shore forgotten in the spread
of dark, the footsteps disappearing in the sand. It might have crossed
your mind the setting sun is an old woman no one knows who moves
through any place she pleases, eyes on everything, nothing that
is hers, always departing, fanfares silent as they follow her

into the dark. Now she is gone forever, darkness is her last
remove, and we are left behind no more remembered than the stones
upon the shore. Elegies must begin here, taking their pace
from her recession: birds move slowly after her until they are
the merest spots of dust beneath the clouds and then are gone, and we
are all seeing, our eyes open with a longing that the sun
departing gives us gazing on, our bodies birds that are the dust.

SONGS

The sleep of birds is music made of dreams exhaled upon the wind
not long before the coming of the sun, of dreams without shape
that spill into the air, a music made of echoes that cannot
recall the songs from which they came—music unheard, music without
a name that makes the air more fugitive, the darkness that contains
it farther apart, music rising from stars that are the universe
as it breathes out an emptiness that spreads into the seas of air

where all the elements that are of dreams rise up and disappear,
their traces brief cadenzas, little songs that fall so carelessly
through one another, fragments of them settling on our bodies as
we sleep, becoming all that lies between us and the open of
the stars, the deeper dark they carry with them in their rising, that
remembrance of the nothing that was theirs before they took their place
as stars we cannot see, illuminating songs that echo air.

DUST

So close we are to being dust again, no stronger than the leaf
that in the harshest summer winds resists, but in an evening late
in fall, when not a breath of wind disturbs the air, is gone, and if
you are awake, the moment that it settles on the ground, the air
leaps back, the silence broken, time ending then, the moment alone
without an end, the dust of it at home in you, your ear attuned
to its eternity. If we are made for dust, it is the dust

of ordinary music hanging in the air and always on
the barest edge of being heard, a dust that cannot play without
our being close to it, so intimate with dust that when it is
invisible in us it plays what silence plays where all that has
departed dances on invisible recesses of the sun. We are
so close to dust that we cannot but be the music that we think
we hear, eternal music of the sun that sets in us, the fall

of evenings resting on our hands, and through them echoes of a leaf,
of children running through the fading light, unable in the dark
to tell the child from the leaf, to tell whose hand it is that holds
the naked sounds that float apart into the greater distance of
the sky where all the dust that has been known lies down and with the stars
comes out, the dark alive as we suppose we are, becoming then
the sky, the sky where we have always been at home, beside the sun.

SMILE

You raised your hand in sudden recognition toward the stillness of
the sky and not a sound escaped your lips, the mere ghost of a smile
taking shape upon them. No one saw what you were able to see—
someone you had known when you were young who passed in such a light
at evening, just before the stars appeared, a bird that had become
so familiar the way it glided was enough to know it, or
the ending of a sentence that had risen in your mind before
the weight of sentences had fallen over you, a sentence so

full of the light of its beginning it had lifted off into
another evening to reside among the stars, an aura that
precedes their coming, not forgotten but unable to call back,
and so it comes of its accord, yet not as you had murmured it
but as a light unburdened, its sense unclear, falling on your face
as rain that falls that is not felt as rain, only its falling known,
the meaning of it beyond sense—the only way to greet it is
with that ghost of a smile that knows the coming of the stars and dark.

COLLAPSING

Something collapses in the early afternoon, as if the sky
fell back into itself, the clouds left over, sun and moon and stars
departed, gone to universes somewhere else, the traces of
the birds no longer visible. There can be now no means to tell
when the evening might come and when to sleep and when to wake.
If there were clocks, there would be holes in them and coming close there would
be no escape—we would fall into them, the time that measured us

a mere abyss where we would pass what memories there were, each one
suspended for a moment, bright before they vanish, elements
of memory all that might be known, their air, their fire, water and
their earth the all that is. What else is there to carry walking near
the clouds remaining by our sides? This is our us, the rest
the disappearing simulacra of a world barely known,
our hands the fire sleeping slowly in the centre of the sun.

PALINGENESIS

When we returned, it seemed that other trees were standing on the round
horizons, birds were clinging to their branches that could not be known
to us, the brightness of their eyes resilient in the morning sun,
all of them—the birds, the trees and branches—etched against the sky
that we had never seen but recognized, the way they stood without
the barest motion given us in its eternity that was
beside us in the light, and people walked beneath them, faces filled

with their intent, unknown to us and known at once. There can be no
before to this, no afterward, horizons all there are where they
arrive and then depart like us, knowledge of what impels them not
within their ken, being the earth and what the earth remembers, its
returns against the sun the larger echo of the change of trees,
everyone walking underneath them with the certainty they are
forever here, the transience of stars engraved upon their brows.

DIALOGUE

Alchemies of autumn are nearly within our grasp where trees rise up
and turn toward the sun, each of them singing gloria, and in
the sun their glories are transmuted, coming back to hang upon
the air, the air suspended in the falling sun, its light upon
us and the song, and all the stones that lie against our feet refined
so surely that the purest sound of stones begins to rise, so soft
the burden of their song is all that light might be where light amid

the dust of leaves arrives, refrains of stone and leaf that utter us,
a world that in its silence speaks, its fiat what the stone and leaf
in singing are, and we are without words, the we we are a place
infinity stands up, and from our mouths its light goes forth: we have
no other song than what the sun supplies and what the stones give back,
a song that only the trees hear, becoming fire in their brief
finalities, and we are given this, to be the spoken light.

ARIA

The stars could not be seen when we came down to the sea, only sounds
of barely falling water in our ears, a sudden passing of
a bird, darkness ignited by the brevity of cries where they
at random seek to find where they have gone, and through the fitful calls
they make you speak, your words rising into the air to join the sighs
of birds, the dark an aria that falls in small rains upon
the sea and us, and intermittent in the music what you said

became an answer that did not appear from you but something that
the dark alone could make, nothing belonging to the birds or us.
Darkness must be entered slowly and without regret, the words
with which we clothed ourselves abandoned, putting on the rain for skin,
our bones a music we have never heard: let them speak us, the gift
of darkness rising up in our breath where birds in passage are
at home, coming and going, naked music left upon the sea.

FIGURES

Two figures in a landscape walking in a rain, keeping a pace
almost the same—they pause to gaze at things seen only by themselves,
and from a distance all the shapes that they configure take the form
of slow enigmas, each outline of their statements bold in their
unfolding, but the insides blurred, and in their distant rain they must
be only figures in a dream that are no more when one of us
awakens. Nothing touches them, the rain before them giving way
as they inside it do not merely walk but on occasion dance

in steps that seem unknown to us, and if asleep you had called out
to them, it could not be that they would hear, the only voices in
their ears their own, the only music sounds of rain against their feet
falling for them. Without them we are not, and when we think of rain,
it is not possible unless the rain is theirs, and should we wake without
the memory of any sudden turn that they might take, all that we
might think we know would fall from us, the world before us but without
form, the rain impossible to grasp, or us or sleep or dream.

COSMOS

The angels came and went, and we remained, only the auras of
the stars suggesting what they might have been, and certain birds that stand
upright upon the edges of the world, unmoving and their eyes
without the fire one expects of angels burning with divine
commands, or they are here but not for us to see, passing beside
us, burdened with what holiness befalls them, or it is that we
would have to be what children are to see them suddenly stand up

before us unbelievable against the sun eclipsed, their light
the only radiance and all the rest in darkness: could we bear
to be surrounded so, the night the one eternity where we
might fall, the only gravity their eyes holding the night we would
become, the words they speak irrevocable music that assumes
the shape of what is uttered. If your name were spoken, you would be
what had been said, and where, and how, a you and cosmos absolute.

APPEARANCES

Certain trees appear upon horizons not as trees but in
the shape of light where shadows pass and disappear, and it cannot
be said where in the mind they take root. There must be birds among
their branches, songs rising into the air, but they are hardly to
be heard: they are the light as music in a distance, coming from
a future whose arrival is without warning—perhaps a note
that stands alone against the sky before it sets, what looks to be

a branch that with its leaves breaks up the light, a branch of shadows that
remembers darkness long enough for darkness to grow into trees
where we with slower movements find our way. How is it possible
for us to be in any other way but standing here where they
in our horizons stand and with them come into the darkness now
and then as shafts of light, the little that we see of them the bare
shape of what we know of us, horizons that at random touch.

UNSEEN

Your hands were resting on a chair, asleep and quiet in their dreams,
the air upon them so absorbed that it appeared unable to
resist, falling into the deeper cadences of where your hands
had gone, and so the air and so your hands began to dream the dream
of earth, the long seasons your fingers moved among the fragile roots
of flowers, holding silence in its tender compass, lifting it
into the air, the moments of it standing up around you in

the shapes of stars that had not yet approached the skies, the figures that
they took almost invisible but each of them enough to make
the air around you seem another heaven where the birds returned
smaller than those we knew before, possessed of music that spreads out
upon the air among the stars almost asleep. The music that
they make comes over us at any moment unannounced, and we
are never sure if this is music or a change of light so swift

its passage, leaving nothing after but a sense of music: so
are stars behind the sun made known to us, as stars that are so near
they are a part of our breath as we exhale, the light of them
unseen. Why do we believe that our eyes behold the world
when without the stars falling around us all that is withheld
from our sight would not be known, the dark but dark, the earth that holds
your hands but earth, the sky turning blindly though the night without a breath?

FACES

Nothing clothes our bodies, we are always naked to ourselves,
our faces signs of what we are, and even in the darkness they
are dimly lit and open to the merest breath, the light that falls
upon them passing through the window—stars and moon, the falling snow—
and all of them leave traces there against the silence lying on
your face, a skin of silence lying there possessed by all passage,
so transparent it must be akin to air, and rising in

it are the trees that stood above your house, their flowers the shape the light
takes before it fades, a face composed of echoes of a light
of flowers falling through stars. There is no other history
but what comes into sight on its horizons—not flowers but how
they were, their going in us all that we can be, and it lies on
us so lightly it might be a nirvana in its coming to us, its
proximity unseen, a world in flower laid bare in us.

WALKING

The rain converses with itself in slow cadences, not
like us bent on finding sense but grander, noting everything
with equal weight, and all that answer—leaves, the small ponds, and grass—
reply from dark reserves of silence, as if it were a god that calls,
and nothing else is heard, the birds absolutely mute, and if
there were any movement, it was you, a rain that walks, your steps
leaving behind no other mark than what the grass gives up in answer,
music of ponds passing by. The birds that hang unmoving on the air

attend your steps, the murmur of the silence standing up before
it disappears invisible inside their eyes, whatever place
you pass the measures of a story theirs alone to read as it
arises from the grass, from deeper in the earth, all its darkness
open for them, the song that they compose a song of silence full
of rain unable to be sung, but all of its divinity
contained: they wait until the grass gives up, and when they sing,
every *the* that they bring forth falls slowly on the earth exact as rain.

TRACES

We saw that we had almost crossed the field, and we were straying near
its farther edges where the trees rose up against a cloudless sky.
We were so far away we did not seem to move, and all our steps
that stretched across the snow away from where we stood were visible
but merged with others, traces of the rabbits, dogs, and smaller beasts
that are forever passing over fields and out of sight. But we
were still within our eyes, if smaller than we think ourselves to be,
and joined to us behind where we were standing, figures in the place

where memories are left, just as we were before we walked across
the field of snow that stretched between what we remembered, if it came
to mind, a field that had no marks but tracks of animals that had
already vanished, traces they had left now settled into us
remembering the all—the field, the snow, the lines of steps, the trees, the all
that falls in us as snow might fall if it were falling back into
the sky and into that infinity that is what we, when we
fall into memory, must be, and there, where snow arises and

the shapes that animals are thought to have, where trees against the sky
are first conceived, the trees that shed upon us all the silence that
is all they have to give, and all of it assumes the shapes we are
for us to be, the shape of silence straying near eternity
where it has come and gone. What are we, then, as we remember us
where our steps across the field go out of sight, and no one there
to tell what vanished in the snow, or what infinity it is
that holds our tracks and all the others near the trees, the cloudless sky?

TEARS

If planets could see, they would avert their gaze, the fires
of the sun would be invisible, and where the moon would rise
an emptiness would move against the sky. Even infinity
would pass away unable in the dark to stand around us. So
the tears of God fall. Nothing can bear to know that he might weep,
their traces unrecorded as they pass, but when they reach the earth,
they settle in the broken flesh of children who are left behind

when all the guns of war have come and gone and night and silence stand
beside them. Our earth is their flesh and in it where the tears
have fallen roses stand in darkness, no one seeing them, and each
holds up the darkened sun, the vacant moon, and all the planets that
now are unable in their grief to look. No infinity
is ours. We have given it away, and in the silence earth
cannot be heard, its music fallen in the night that covers us.

EVERYWHERE

All the trees that stand along the world's horizon seem to be
no more than trees, but when you stand beneath them they take in the light
from what you think to be the sun, and in the absence of the sun
the moon, and when the moon has set and nothing spreads across the sky
but darkness and the memory of light, a light that settles in
the trees, and at their feet the stones appear to open, smaller moons
that bear the smallest light where darkness falls across the ground. If God
is everywhere, then he is here in this passage where you have stopped,

but it is God that is the simplest tree that bears the air alone
above itself, and all that moves within its compass stands within
that large divinity of all that passes. Nothing seems so swift:
horizons are so close they could be resting on your hands, the sun behind
them, moving without rest, impossible to tell the darkness from the light,
and if you turned around, the world would have turned with you, the stones
against your feet appearing not to change, the light that animates
their being stone rising toward the trees and farther toward the sky,
its passage the tree and you, horizons on their branches turning green.

DRIFTING

The smell of lilacs drifts from room to room. It carries summer on its breath,
but summers that have come and gone, all the summers that were full
of our childhoods asleep inside the drifting smell, and so
invisible that you might say that they are in their paradise,
the sudden cries that sprang into the air beneath the trees the cries
that now are heard, drifting along where lilacs in the dusk appear
so near I thought they grew beside the window, overflowing through
the air. How can we breathe without the breath of childhood, the cries

that rush among the leaves, their taking of the world, the stars that fill
their eyes, the innocence that sheathes their bodies, childhood that is
its own eternity where nothing enters but itself? But what
it is—no more than breath—is to be held, this paradise where they
go up into the summer, lilac air, disappearing just
as they take shape, the air becoming echoes of itself, and if
we are reborn, it is in voices we have never spoken, each
rising in us to rest upon our breath, lilacs in us surprised.

SKIES

In the middle of a field there stood a house that had been left
behind many years before we passed that way. The light that filled
it passed unhindered through the windows: you could always see the sky
which it contained inside it everywhere, a house before it fell
already of the sun. A little road went past it falling toward
a river where in autumn you could almost cross by stepping on
the stones. Such streams are made for dreaming, and when summer lay upon
it, light flowed over it and left a trace of sky dappled upon

it, clear enough to know the house and stream were kin, places where
the sky came down, always at home, the moon pausing there, so near
it cannot be the stars are only in a distance far too far for us
to touch. The sky is everywhere, unmoved by how we see, and what
appear as banks of streams, the shores of seas, the humblest, falling walls—
this is where the sky comes up to us, and then, in what appears to be
the summer dreaming, we are wakened seeing we are shores, but shores
without an edge, and resident where planets pass invisible.

AIR

And so the colour of the air is the colour of the sea when it
in absolute transparency wells up before our eyes, the clouds
the only waves, and all that comes in sight is what eternity
holds up, the sound of it inaudible and lapping at our skin.
How close we are to nothing here, smaller than all that you might think
is small, the earth against our feet the larger shore, but held in its
immensity? The gods can barely see us standing here, our arms
extended barely on the edges of infinity. We think

we have been born: we leap, we run, we leave each other in our wakes,
and in the air, if you were standing on the moon, nothing would
appear. And so perhaps we have not yet been born, but dream ourselves
into the world, no divinity in the forever of
the air having knowledge of us, and so we dream the gods that they,
when they begin to dream, imagine it is we who are the folly
filling them, but their eyes, if they are gods, only the shape
of immortality take in, the rest unnoticed like the air.

PETALS

Her death has entered you, her death that has become relentless in
undying life. It is a flower that untouched by snow endures—
of snow and that air that falls pitiless through the winter dark,
where petals slip away in silence, impossible to tell if they
are snow or if the snow deceived stands up beneath the air, between
one horizon and another the only flower visible.
No one arrives to gather it, to grasp the flowered air, and so
it stands, nodding under the wind. The darkness pauses, standing near,

the whiteness of the flower light that darkness cannot overcome.
And so you have become the one to bear this flower that resists
the dark, unable to abandon flowering, to fall unseen
inside the snow. It is a light that has no name, no one can call
to it across the wind. Horizons lose their place. If it found
its way there, how would it know where it arrived, the only light
around, the sun obscured behind the falling snow, the compass of
the dark taking shape from it, a small cosmos consumed?

SHADOWING

Our shadows stretched across the freshly fallen snow so far it seemed
to reach the near horizon, falling into frozen ponds and rising
to the fields that followed: all that was left was what the moon gave off,
the air as far as we might see largesse of light that filled our eyes,
and breathing through our flesh that stood between the moon and snow, a flesh
of light surrendered. Creatures walking through it were not possible
to see as other than the moon in other guises, and the shadows that

they cast dissolve into themselves across the snow, the lives we thought
were theirs possessing what the moon possesses—nothing final in
their shapes and flowing over in the light with shade that hovers near
the ground impalpable. We must be them, the shades they cast and ours
a breath our bodies exhale, ways of talking, then, with no more sound
than snow contains against the ground where we are standing, each of us
a phase of shadow, snow, the moon, our lives not known but otherwise.

IMMENSITY

Unperceived the moon appeared against a starless sky and paused
before it disappeared behind the clouds. No one remembered where
its rising was. Its immensity was there before us, no other
thing to know but darkness and the sound that emptiness can make,
the nothing of the clouds, the moon departing, or immensity
that when it settles in the mind is all immensity and what
it brings—God, perhaps, before he spoke the world, at home in all
the nothing that there is, who spoke and nothing came to be. And so

the moon is not forgotten, in us as eternity is in
us, and the stars invisible. It is not death that enters us:
it is the moon alive in its immensity arising from
the nothing no one saw, filling the sky and entering the clouds,
ours in that instant that dilates across the moment we
are given. This is what forever that there is, its light in us
given forever as it passes, nothing overflowing with
the moon, all the stars turning round us but where they are unknown.

OFFERING

Eternities are without weight. Distance fills the smallest stone.
The light moves across it, day by day, the night full of changing
moons, the rains that wash it, emptiness that deepens with the wind.
It does not live in time, but you can lift it, grasp the fullness of
it in your hand. If God were capable, he would hold it out
to you, and holding it, it would be more than stoniness inside

your hand, and all that it possesses—gravity, the fall that moves
across the light, and God the falling, falling through the distance that
spills over your fingers—settled between the stone and where your hand
appears to hold it. Only we can offer it to God, and all
the falling that we are is given back. It is the way we have
of turning homeward when the stars appear above to rise in us.

GIFT

All is gift: a solitary bird that sings invisible
among the leaves, and singing so to offer up the spring and lay
it on the threshold of your ears, a child whose gaze is steady through
the windows of the world, rain unbidden falling on the glass,
your hand that lies beside you open taking in what passes through
the air. Whatever moves is known as all that is unknown, and so
the darkness rests upon your flesh both intimate and never grasped,
and all that might be named, the blades of grass and pebbles lying near

your feet, the patient stars and passages of birds, your breathing that
takes in the air and gives it back, people who stand beside the sea
to see the waves come into shore and disappear, no one can say—
not children nor the singing bird that stands apart beyond all sight—
why this occurs and how it all occurs again in us, the world
passing through our eyes to be reborn and then exhaled, but all
of us are nothing other than what stands a moment in the air
beside the sun that moves forever past, no sun at all but us.

SINGING STONES

When the moon upon its long horizons lay, the clouds around
it stood so full and white you might have thought the world at last had stopped,
rivers ceased to flow in their beds, among the branches of the trees
heaven spread out, and little stones that had fallen upon the ground
and held inside them all the silence of the world began to keen,
the music that they make so clear and high it does not sound as music
you had heard, but as the snow would feel, falling with rain when it

comes sudden in the spring across a large expanse of air. There is
no way outside of this, the moon possessing all, rising larger
and larger across the mind, its horizons those the moon lies down
upon, the stars invisible, only the moon and night inside
us taking shape, the darkness flowing through us, welling from the heart
of all that is without a touch of light to rise beside the moon
and move where it would move, our bodies where it dwells, the mind the moon.

FIRE BIRDS

A rowan tree was standing in its final fires, burning through
the long autumnal rains, so sheathed in its mortality you thought
its death a beauty overcoming all abandon, yet perhaps
it is the bush where God chose once to speak, and speaking still becomes
the bush in its finality, the leaves surrendered to the air,
the birds that perch among its berries drinking in the words that have
no clearer shape than this and knowing God unable to be heard,

but all are turned toward the tree, attentive, each refusing to
depart, belonging to the bright mortality in which they stand,
and one cries out and then another, fire flowing in their mouths,
the God they know the God they turn to song, mortality alive
upon their tongues, the music fire that we see about us, the flames
the one divinity that we are given going back into
the air without the residue of ash, fire leaping and gone.

SISTERS

After a while the little bust upon the shelf began to look
like you. Rain did not change the look upon her face, but sometimes in
the twilight, her eyes would sink into themselves, eyes that are no more
than hints of eyes that stare unfocussed into air. Around her head
her hair is shaped like yours, in curls that recall a sea so small
it could be held and contemplated anywhere. Beneath the moon
the alabaster of her skin, so perfect even death could sleep

beside it, comes alive, her face a smooth eternity where sadness
lurks, no star untouched by how she gazes on them, absence in
her eyes that settles everywhere the air, as if a memory
were opened, breathes. A simple bow completes her blouse: Could it be
that if eternity were seen, it would reveal itself to be
a bow that clasped all in its simplicity, too modest to
appear companion to the sun, content with darkness on a shelf?

TREE

Nothing lay beneath the tree but snow, the air more barren than
the ground where traces of an animal that had departed stayed.
The moon hovered over the tree, its light too cold to thaw the frost
upon its branches, but light lay on them and they shone barely, the sky
behind it closed, a thin candelabra without flame. It was
impossible for you standing near to touch it: more of sky
it seemed than anything the earth could offer up. And so, as if

to speak to it, you were overcome by tears, by tears that seemed
to come upon you from the highest sky and from the tree that rose
against it, tears that fell as frozen rain upon your face and rolled away
upon the snow, their silence without trace upon the ground. The tree
did not move, but bareness lay upon it, the absolute of all
bareness, nothing between the sky, the tree, and you, the tears that fell
falling away beyond the snow upon the dark, the nothing of air.

RIFT

I saw your soul sit down and weep. Nothing that was beside you that
did not fall into silence, all familiar but all apart,
the sun another sun and in another sky, the nearest tree
and flower near but always out of reach, and nothing there is what weeps
with you. A rift has opened in the air just at the point where tears
cannot be heard, and on the other side all there is goes on
impelled to be the only thing it is. The flower opens, rain

falls from the cloud and grass stands patiently waiting all across
the world. Deepest in the silence, pebbles hold whatever is
not said. The rift does not close, and everywhere your weeping through
the air extends the world opens and, unnoticed as the snow
that falls past a sightless eye, cold and darkness gather shape,
lying together with the smallest stones, silence becoming breath
and rising from them through the world, and on it sun and moon afloat.

SHADES

May they come slowly, the long shades of night, no bird surprised
but altering the light from infinite to infinite until
it comes to rest upon your hands and you might see it lie as stones
lie down beneath untroubled waters where quietly the fish
together float in sleep, and air upon the grass is still. The earth
is born there in that darkness you have touched asleep upon

your flesh, and there the rivers stand, the trees across its surface move,
and all the stories you had heard in childhood, of creatures great
and small, dissolve from word to flesh, the air transformed into a sigh—
o wordless turning of the earth alive inside the darkness of
your hands, everything turning with the new sun, the smaller fires
of the stars igniting the skies, the dark dumbfounded and alive.

TRACKS

Coming back across the snow, we turned and saw our tracks behind
us, slight impressions that grew smaller as they stretched invisible
into the distance, quickly being dashed away where dogs ran back
and forth along the point where we had stepped away from trees, or were
they merged with other tracks as someone telling stories pauses, then
begins another and the track of one is taken by the new
one? By the time the field is crossed, deer may walk across the steps
we claimed as ours, and no one could distinguish us from deer except

perhaps by looking at the way our feet were shaped. But when we walk in such
a way that we enter each other, where is that expanse of snow
where we might measure where we thought we had begun, how far it was
that we had moved? The stories that we seem to be now cannot
have lost what might have prefaced them—impossible to track the way
they turn toward the suns that move across the skies at will, but if
they are in some way kept, it is the dark that holds them all, and what
it knows it knows without the ignorance of words that flutter in

the air, each a bird that cannot see, and able but to sigh,
then fall and disappear, but darkness keeps the rest—your eyes that are
open in eternity, that in their look carries what is not
to be believed, but is, a look that has beheld the sun inside
itself, where all the light that is suddenly is, and in that light
the keeping of all beginnings and all ends and where they meet, and when
the snow begins to fall, its beginning is in that light
that floats across the world and waits. There without a word we move.

BARED

Shadows of a birch tree lay effortlessly on the snow,
and in that instant there was nothing like it, it contained the all
the tree and shade and light could be, and if a bird were singing, it
would not have been perceived. Only the air in passing could disturb
that perfection that they made—or time or sun or cloud—or one
glance aside, and looking back it could be seen that what there was
of shade had changed, no longer clear, the shape the tree had cast now blurred,

the blue that had in layers lifted through the air departed. Then
it was I heard your voice, a voice that came from distances outside
the shade the tree gave up, a wordless voice that hovered in the air
that now remains, a voice that if visible would be air that falls
layer by layer, air you could put on, and all that could be seen
would be an afterward of what the tree had given, after shade
and after light, an afterward that lies upon the least thing

and nothing changed—the stones that were before in place upon the ground
exactly as they were. Only the air has changed, the naked sound
it makes of music that, when it moves, enfolds, and where it is
nothing else—the barest tree, the stones—can recognize itself,
gathered into itself. There there is no afterward, the sun
the all of light, the tree the all of form against the air, the stones
the all of silence, music the all of absence in an instant filled.

DANCED

Each where they have been appointed take their places, stars that in
their distance seem no other than the merest points of light against
the coming of the dark, and there they pause, at first uncertain if
that is all to which they have been called—to be a light without
light, markers that come and go, unable to withstand the sun,
but in the dark that settles on the sea, the light that they give off
begins to move, their light a sudden offering to water that
removes from them the order that they know against the sky, to be

the grave simplicities the stories of the world cast upon them, gods
that lost and goddesses whose only home is air, and now, returned
to where they had begun, they dance unthinking on the sea, the sea
appearing everywhere illumined with a light abandoned so
without its solitary godliness, only water and
a memory of fire, the stars afloat, the water burning through
the night. Perhaps you think you stand upon a shore, as if to bear
witness to all that moves before you, gods that have become the light

and gods that have been cast from their divinity, and think the sea
merely the sea and stars ghosts of themselves, but none is capable
of bearing witness, the shore is no more shore than gods are gods. For you
there is no place to move but into water, to be there the dance
that is in you and in the stars, no up, no down, no east, no west,
no other godliness than this to bear, of water filled with light
and stars that slip across your flesh, what flesh you are a flesh without
the weight of flesh: movement is all, the giving up a taking in.

PICTURES

The darkness came first, a shade that fell across the pictures that
did not belong to them, but came from everything around, the dark
that hung upon the air, the sun forgotten, pictures of the dark that held
the darkness seen and darkness known, the darkness painted now
alive again but not for anyone to grasp, yet being in
the air you know its passage crossing through your flesh unable to
remain, the way that crows advance inexorable across a field
and then retreat, taking their darkness back, but some, a slower dark,

linger behind, their shade hastily neglected, a harvest that
has not been gathered, winter come too soon, premonitory but
without a sign, the absence that it bears a falling taken in
but not comprehended, the life we are the shades that fall without
our knowing over flesh we take as ours, a destiny to wear
until it is what must remain of us, the slow dark that waits
to gather us, waiting in rooms we had forgotten, rooms that held
us once and let us go, but always present, winter air to breathe.

AFTERNOON

We were hanging pictures in the afternoon, pictures that were
of places we had never seen and times that were long gone, but we
had seen them often in one another's rooms that had grown so
familiar we could almost think that we had been in every place
before, stepping behind the trees of parks where people walked in their
ceremonious clothes, where carriages and horses passed, but passed
without the slightest movement toward an absent sky, their afternoons

more lasting than the ones beyond their reach. And so we carry them,
our hands the traces of what was to come for them, vanishing points
that find in us their coming and their going, full of what they were
apart from us, flowers that are forever open, openness
in us at rest. We are the afternoons, their passing and the still
eternities possessing them, the parks, the people walking through
their silence almost reaching us, the air an echo of amens.

PEBBLES

Now there is a bluejay on the fence, his eyes so bright against
the sun that nothing in his sight escapes his knowledge, all that lies
before him so clear he seems to read his mind as he absorbs
what falls around him: berries, leaves, the rays of light the sun sends forth,
pebbles that no one knows are there, almost invisible pebbles that are
the dream of pebbles before they are that rest unmoved upon the edge
of flight. Perhaps you have heard people praying in the night, the words

they speak confused, a borderland where languages converse without
knowledge of what is said, but all spoken perfectly, and each
is giving shape to worlds that they know, and each alone in its own
purity of line. What do their prayers carry but what they are,
unfolding into night, and when they stop in silence, God is that
place where they stop, but God as in the shape of pebbles lying on
the edges of the earth, of pebbles undreamt and waiting in the dark?

FIELD

A stream emerged in front of us and on the other side a field,
sleeping in the early sun, the grass not yet awake or trees,
and birds suspended in the air. All of it began to take
a semblance of a shape within our eyes: the colours entered first
and found a place, and in them what was there resumed, the birds within
the air within our eyes and still above the trees. We crossed the stream
and stepped into the field and did not notice how at first the air
began to change, the air much closer to our breath than any air

in any field, and then it was we saw some distance in the field
the shapes of children coming toward us, two alone who walked beneath
the trees, the field now wakened from its slumber, two who seemed like you
and me, but you and me before we knew who you and me had been,
and they were walking slowly side by side not looking where they walked
yet knowing every moment where they were. We wondered how it might
be possible to speak to them, for then we noticed everything
within the field was silent, all that we could hear was our breath,

and nothing seemed to move but them and birds that were within their wake.
Neither of us recalled if we had seen the sun above the birds,
but light there was, and it was streaming down along their silent flesh
and on the birds, their only element the light, and when they moved,
the light was moving where they moved, impossible to know who was
the light and who was not, the sound of our breath the sound of light.
We turned toward each other, looking into our gaze, and what
we saw was nothing of our look and of our eyes, but all there was

of fire rising from our bodies, fire that was of itself
and what it knew of fire falling from the sun, a fire that
was only fire. We must be the fire, and what we recall
is fire in itself, its childhood of fire somewhere else
and fire that is still of fire now, the past of fire its
eternity in us, and if I touch you, what I touch is me,
yet me not standing in the fire, being God within a bush,
but me in you and you the fire, our breath a childhood

unknown to us that we have seen emerging from the sun to move
within our flesh in rhythms that are those of our primal breaths
when we took in the that that made us us, the breath that was the light
that radiated through the field, the grass, the trees, the children who
were moving there and moving through the fire that we breathed, their breath
the first of fire in our mouths, divinity invisible,
and is the we we see when we behold the fire where we are,
incapable of age, the is of everything that is of us.

FOLLOWING

It seemed as if you walked across a field, walking forever past
the things the field contained—the trees, the ponds, the little stones that lie
beside your path, your feet noting only the grass. Mountains in
their distances rise up and disappear in clouds, no more concerned
than birds that pass, dissolving in the air, and I walk always behind,
the steps I take stumbling into words, a word for ponds, for trees,
and all the things that take their place around you, a whole world that comes
and goes and left in silence on a page, and the air moves around

you as you pass, an air that rises without being seen into
the clouds that form the base of what we call the heavens where you walk
at night against the moon, the words that lie here in sequence the path
you leave behind, and everything before you places that cannot speak:
impossible to say if God is there, a sun that never sets,
the stars invisible until they have been passed, one after
the other, each becoming word, and their eternities a field
composed of ponds, of little stones, the sounds of feet upon the grass.

NORTH

For some, a star is all there is, alone and without motion in
a cloudless sky, silently setting forth the order of the sun
and moon, no other centre visible. Without it, music would
not turn upon itself. Where would the stones fall, if they were about
to fall, or streams descend, or oceans—all unmoving in their tracks?
And so it rests there, infinitesimal polaris that
is lord, and once in place even God could turn his back and say,
'It is done,' and enter his eternal sabbaths satisfied.
And so it's possible to pray, merely holding it in sight,
and knowing that what knowledge we might need is open in its light,

the sun too hasty, every moon a fickle child, the other stars
but light that merely dazzles, light that falls apart upon the seas
and streams. If any, then, were lost, unsure what turn to take or how
to choose, what other light would lead to right or left, illuminate
the shade that falls on everything that lives, o light that holds the dark
in darkness, light that in the slightest breath is all that breathes, o light
that is the night speaking when it appears, the words it forms, the words
that mother every other word that can be known, their falling through
the air invisible to settle in the voice, and so without
the least awareness, all that's spoken falls from farthest north unheard.

But we who dwell in our north, where is the north that we might call
upon and name the north, the north not there secure in all the space
it has been given, no one near it who might take that absent star
in hand, that star that makes of absence all the compass that is known?
For us, the grass beneath our feet is north, the nearest tree, and if
you should bend down and touch the ground, the north is there, your fingers stretched
upon it, nothing firmer, a north, then, that never goes away,
its seasons appearances of passage, winter its one habit where
whatever is must be, winter its true imperative, all else—
the thought of suns warming the sea, the sun itself, fire and

a light that rests at home upon the flesh where you might stroll unclothed
even at night, the world given for nothing but langour—all else
not other, the fine south of longing and desire, not other than
the thinnest thread of thought, a thought so ephemeral you can
not think that it was thought, and so when winter leaves, its parting is
its best deception, sinking merely from sight to wait beneath the ground,
our feet never far from snow, the brighter air, the sound that seems
to have lost breath. North is not a place, a star to which we turn
when we are lost. The north where we forever dwell is everywhere,
its embrace without the possibility of loss, and all

that is is north, the difference between us, then, incapable
of being found, no star to see. How do I tell you, then, that we,
walking side by side in this immeasurable space, are
the star that is the gravity that gives measure to all that falls,
to all that would leap up and sing into the emptiness that lies
between us and that farthest shore of light, and where does what I say
come from if one star possesses all that can be said, or these,
the smallest stones that lie beside us, where are they if not where they
have been forever, the smallest norths that we might see or hold or know,
our feet stirring the north, north that is but being, its presence ours.

SAYING GOD

Words that are themselves eternity arrive unfathomed in
the mind, the syllables that make them up unable to be held
by you alone and so they spill between us taking shape like whales
that swim beneath the surface of the sea, their backs from time
to time becoming visible. Just parts of words are all that we
are given, words so large that how they might have started is now lost,
floating apart through our childhoods, memories of whales
that may not have been seen, and you might think that all was said when you

in some hour that you have thought the darkest utter God and no
response forms in the air, the air unrippled like a frozen sea:
we, whoever we are, cannot contain such words, and who could write
them down? All we can be are coasts where whales go by singing through
the seas, the echoes of their songs unfolding farther in the dark
than anyone imagines, the echoes of their echoes gathering God
but not by any name, as if it were an autumn in the sea
and all the harvest gleaned and gone, only the singing air left.

HEARING GREEN

Trees in the early morning light stand up and speak in voices so
gentle you may not hear them if you do not lean into the air
surrounding them. Before silence returns, you hear them saying green,
but green in such polyphonies that you are not quite sure what you
have heard, and so you lean again. No one is there to tell you how
to stand, how to move beneath the turns the wind takes, and how
in the slow coming of spring to be the green that you become. There is
no one to tell you how to live. The only life is like a sleep,

and in the sleep a dream that is not yours but is a gift, the gift
a tree that is inside the dream, and in the tree is God and in
God the air and in the air the green. The last inside is you
and here is where the trees stand up and breathe. Eternity cannot
arrive at any faster pace, and when its fullness has become
the fullness that grows large in them, and they are then the green that they
have uttered in the early morning air, then are they the green
where we are given sleep, the green alone standing up to breathe.

ACCOMPANIMENTS

The skies that rise above the villages are larger than
those that over greater towns arrive to stand merely in the dark,
but over villages the stars are everywhere, the brightness of
the sky so full with them that only butterflies might pass between
the space they leave, and in the long succession of the nights they pass
above your head, nothing visible in their wake, just the light
and traces of the darkness that they carry with them. This is all

that you are given, this and how the sound your breathing makes inside
the silence seems to come from something else, not you, not stars, but from
another presence without name, an animal that darkness seems
to set forth, a kind of music that is heard but barely, breath
that when singing enters the world, carries it away, and when
the smallest flowers open, breathing themselves into the space around
them—gardens, ditches along the roads—they float, giving up the souls

that they possess to enter other souls. And so it is not you
and stars that give the world its shape, but just the limits it might have,
and what is left is settled by the air, the that that is the dark
of trees, of grass, of you, given off beneath the stars to hold
them in their course, the shadow that of all shadows no one sees.
So it must be that stars upon the breath of all the night where they
appear are floating on the breathing dark, no other order there.

PRAIRIE

It was a room of pictures of abandoned houses, black and white,
that hung upon the walls. Nothing at first was visible, not trees
or sky: all were one in their thin exhalations of absence, the
remembering that was all the air contained, and what, if not
the coming and the going of the sun, the wind, a word, a look
that had begun without a stumble, gazing boldly at a rock
that stood upright against the ground and saw the night gradually fill
the space between the eye and what lay still before it—then it was

the world could not be but shades of grey, the white of sky that through
the weathered wood seemed no more than paper that had given up
its story of the moon no longer to be heard against the walls
of failing barns, the bones that were partially covered by the ground,
memories of bones that might have been the bones of anything
that had lain there and never moved again, immobile underneath
a sky that did not move. You could not bear the place, even in black
and white, where if you looked into the sky, no bird was there, nor star—

and each time your eye went past the scenes that stood around you, what
was there to fill your eyes but infinite gestures of removal, each
too small to see alone, but gathered they began to hover in
the room around you, a breath that did not move up against your flesh,
but drew away, an absence that opened at touch, and when you saw
it, you could not speak, the air inside your mouth drawn away, the taste
of bare mortality left behind, a taste that had no taste
but what greyness brings or nothing, holes where stars have fallen through.

WIND

It has begun to snow again, falling indifferently, a kind
of Buddhist snow, you might have said, that has a music running through
it with an aimless rhythm, heard but not attended to, where you
or anyone might wander, walking fitfully on sleeping grass,
no stars as guides, the sun behind the clouds, and when birds appeared,
they blew apart, the circles that they formed never complete but each
opening, closing only to dissolve, the air remembering

their absence here and there. The snow settles briefly on your hair:
before melting, my eyes are seized by its instant of eternity
that falls carelessly into time. Beside it we are nothing but a place
where wind blows through at night, an anywhere that might be known to birds
if they are blown there too. Without it there is no northern star, no
knowing of music and its aimlessness that rises and descends
transparent through the air remembering what falls not ours to see.

WAKES

Then what are we but fragments of a larger word, not syllables
or letters, just a sound that has not yet come into being that
the merest breath of air might overcome? Ponds are more when they
wait for passing showers, a drop of rain falling far away
that settles on the water's surface open blankly to the sky,
and so it is suddenly there, a tear flowing backward to pause
and leave a little wake before it disappears, the lake unmoved
apparently and giving nothing up, nothing occurring but

the other wake that flows across your mind, unable to possess
the slightest sense of what has happened in the air and after on
the lake that gives up nothing but the sky, its semblance and the shape
of absence. Are we then where wakes are written without trace, the thin
circles that they make minuscule echoes of the moments when
we think it might have been the rain in passing or a fish that came
too near the air and then retreated, giving up the slightest breath,
the tear we thought we saw, the rain or fish opening a lake?

SCREAM

In the night you screamed. All the time that moved around us stopped,
and when you screamed, it did not spread into the space that time had left
but stood, a single shaft of light that wavered barely at the top.
The light it casts puts everything around into shade, the stars
that we remember growing dimmer in its light, and if we lift
our hands, we see that they are only shadows moving through the air
that drift among the other shadows of familiar things that have

slipped away into the dark. We do not think to speak, unsure
if words might only be the echoes of the shades that pass without
constraint through air and flesh and stars, the sounds they make a music that
weightless through the darkness rises and falls, but where your scream takes shape
the silence that might hold such music falters, words becoming syllables
that connect at random. It is the world that falters, gods that walked among
the stars with gravity invisible, the dark without form.

TOMBEAU

And so I came, and went into the basement of the church where you
were known, a church whose name was not in any language I had learned,
the pictures on the wall of loss and death and heroism that
had happened long ago, and no one would forget. Beside them you
were also visible, your face as I had seen you last, your eyes
focused on something not in sight behind me, eyes that you have now

carried to another place, wherever you are now, and some
will say that you have gone home, as if you ever had a home
that was not lost somewhere between the language that I heard and all
the languages that floated homeless on your tongue in words that in
the absence that surrounds them echo through the endless afternoons
that follow you. Someday it is possible that we among

the stars may meet in passing. You will speak to me again as you
in our last exchange of words had said that you were on the point
of stopping here and maybe there and there, until it seemed that there
was nowhere you were going to stay, content as one who gazes at
the world passing, nothing becoming yours, at home there without
a word in any alphabet that might settle upon it as yours.

GODS OR

Something was lacking in the whole plan as if you floated in
not one but many mirrors, one casting back a hand, another with
a face, enough to recognize that you were there, but not enough
to see the fit, familiar but without a name, and if you stood
upon the ground, it seemed as if it was not earth beneath your feet,
but something giving way, like snow before compacting in the wind.
If you call out, every word in your head distinct, the sentence that
bursts upon the air is heard as birds might sound if they were in

distress, impossible to grasp, and so it was you came to know
how, if not the gods, then angels might come into being as
the only answer prayer might have, but angels that appear
as early snow, floating across the earth and going out of sight
just as it settles on the ground, as if when they were seen they were
always departing, giving us their purity in instants that
could not be held in our embrace, of gods the only trace that passed
without the certainty of knowing whether they had come at all.

FACES

Nothing clothes our bodies, we are always naked to ourselves,
our faces signs of what we are, and even in the darkness they
are dimly lit and open to the merest breath, the light that falls
upon them passing through the window—stars and moon, the falling snow—
and all of them leave traces there against the silence lying on
your face, a skin of silence lying there possessed by all passage,
so transparent it must be akin to air, and rising in

it are the trees that stood above your house, their flowers the shape the light
takes before it fades, a face composed of echoes of a light
of flowers falling through stars. There is no other history
but what comes into sight on its horizons—not flowers but how
they were, their going in us all that we can be, and it lies on
us so lightly it might be a nirvana in its coming to us, its
proximity unseen, a world in flower laid bare in us.